For my father.

Houghton Mifflin Books for Children is an imprint of Houghton Mifflin Harcourt Publishing Company.

www.hmhbooks.com

The text of this book is set in Gill Sans.
The illustrations are torn- and cut-paper collage.

Library of Congress Cataloging-in-Publication Data

Jenkins, Steve.
  Just a second / Steve Jenkins.
     p. cm.
  ISBN 978-0-618-70896-3 (hardback)
  1. Time—Juvenile literature. 2. Nature—Juvenile literature. I. Title.
  QB209.5.J456 2011
  529—dc22
  2011002104

Manufactured in Singapore
TWP 10 9 8 7 6 5 4 3 2 1
4500305155

JUST A SECOND

SECOND

A DIFFERENT WAY TO LOOK AT TIME

STEVE JENKINS

HOUGHTON MIFFLIN BOOKS FOR CHILDREN • HOUGHTON MIFFLIN HARCOURT • BOSTON NEW YORK 2011

A second goes by pretty quickly. In fact, several have passed since you started reading this sentence. And they just keep going by.

There are 60 seconds in every minute, 3,600 in every hour, and on and on. Most people reading this book will experience more than 2½ billion seconds in their lifetime.

But a lot can happen in a second. Some surprising — even amazing — things can take place in a very short time. Other events unfold more slowly . . .

And that's what this book is about.

In One Second...

A vulture in flight flaps its wings once.

The second doesn't relate to any cycle in nature — it's a human invention, and the shortest interval of time most of us use in our daily lives. The Babylonians came up with the idea of the second about 4,000 years ago, but they had no way to measure such a short interval of time.

A pygmy shrew's heart beats 14 times.

A hummingbird beats its wings 50 times.

A bumblebee beats its wings 200 times.

A midge, a kind of gnat, beats its wings 1,000 times.

A bat can make 200 high-pitched calls.

A woodpecker hammers a tree trunk with its beak 20 times.

A rattlesnake shakes its tail in warning 60 times.

In One Second...

A cheetah sprinting flat out...

A black mamba slithers a frightening 24 feet (7 meters).

...and a sailfish swimming at top speed...

A dragonfly in flight cruises 50 feet (15 meters).

...both travel 100 feet (30 meters).

A very fast human can run 39 feet (12 meters).

A peregrine falcon in a
dive, or stoop, plunges more
than 300 feet (91 meters).

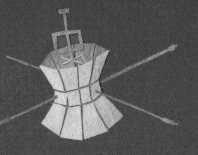

The Helios II satellite
zoomed 43½ miles (70
kilometers). This is the
fastest a man-made object
has ever traveled.

A stone dropped
from rest falls
16 feet (5 meters).

A commercial jet at cruising altitude
covers about 800 feet (244 meters).

The jet-powered Thrust SSC covered
1,119 feet (341 meters) while setting the land-speed record.

In One Second . . .

A meteor entering Earth's atmosphere can travel 44 miles (71 kilometers).

A howler monkey's deafening scream travels 1,125 feet (343 meters).

A human can blink seven times.

A humpback whale's song travels 5,085 feet (1,550 meters) through the water.

Somewhere in the world

Light travels 186,000 miles (300,000 kilometers).

The *Apollo 10* spacecraft traveled almost seven miles (11 kilometers) during reentry — the fastest humans have traveled in a man-made vehicle.

1,500 chickens are killed.

Four babies are born (and two people die).

Earth advances 18½ miles (30 kilometers) in its orbit around the sun.

The male manakin rubs its wing tips together more than 100 times, creating a sound like a note played on a violin.

In One Minute . . .

A person walking at a brisk pace covers about 300 feet (91 meters).

A three-toed sloth hauls itself about ten feet (3 meters).

A giant tortoise lumbers about 15 feet (4½ meters).

The minute, like the second, isn't based on any natural cycle. The sixty minutes in an hour, like the sixty seconds in a minute, are based on a Babylonian counting system that was in use thousands of years ago.

A common snail glides about one foot (30 centimeters) on its slimy track.

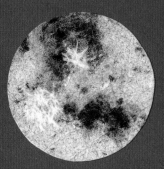

The moon travels 38 miles (61 kilometers) in its orbit around Earth.

A skydiver in free fall plunges two miles (3¼ kilometers).

18 miles (29 kilometers) as Earth rotates.

A person standing in one spot at the equator travels

A charging grizzly bear gallops one half-mile (805 meters).

In One Minute . . .

A very chilly crocodile's heart may slow to just one beat.

A child's heart beats about 100 times.

An adult's heart beats about 70 times.

An elephant's heart beats about 30 times.

A hamster's heart beats about 450 times.

It rained 1½ inches (38 millimeters) on Guadeloupe, an island in the Caribbean — a record.

The world's population increases by 149 people (265 people are born and 116 people die).

A hungry horned lizard can eat 45 ants, one at a time.

2,200,000 pounds (998,000 kilograms) of rice are harvested.

Around the world, 59,000 barrels of oil are used (almost 15,000 of them in the United States).

People around the world drink the equivalent of 2,600,000 twelve-ounce soft drinks.

In One Hour...

An average of 19 gallons (72 liters) of fresh water is used for every person on earth.

15,913 people are born and 6,933 people die. The world's population increases by 8,980.

An adult takes about 900 breaths.

The hour was also created by humans. The hour we use today comes from the Egyptians. About 4,000 years ago, they began dividing the daytime and nighttime each into twelve parts.

A mole can dig a tunnel 20 feet (6 meters) long.

A starfish can crawl 30 feet (9 meters) or more, using the tiny tube feet on its arms.

7,500 pounds (3,402 kilograms) of space debris — most of it dust — falls to Earth.

The sun travels half a million miles (805,000 kilometers) on its trip around the center of the Milky Way galaxy.

A baby blue whale feeding on its mother's milk gains almost ten pounds (4½ kilograms).

In One Day...

Chickens around the world lay two billion eggs.

Kelp, a kind of seaweed, can grow 18 inches (46 centimeters).

A giant anteater can lap up 30,000 termites.

The day is based on the rising and setting of the sun — the time it takes Earth to make one rotation on its axis. The day is the original unit of timekeeping in every human culture.

A mayfly larva hatches, lives its entire life, and dies.

The world's population increases by about 215,000 people (382,000 are born and 167,000 die).

A female flea can lay
100 eggs.

Fifty new species of plants
and animals are identified,
but another 150 species go
extinct, most because of
human activity.

The population of India
increases by 47,000 people.

An adult human
heart beats about
100,000 times.

Bamboo can grow
36 inches
(91 centimeters).

People use the equivalent
of 200 billion sheets of
letter-size paper.

In One Week ...

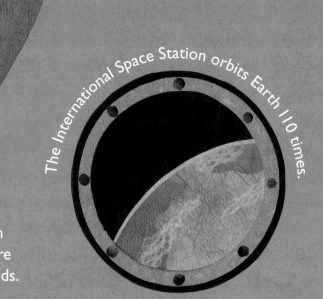

A migrating bar-tailed godwit flies 5,500 miles (8,851 kilometers).

A ladybug can consume more than 500 aphids.

The International Space Station orbits Earth 110 times.

Over the ages, people found it useful to have a unit of time longer than a day but shorter than a month — what we call a week. Weeks have varied in length from three to twenty days. Our seven-day week originated in Babylonia around 2,500 years ago.

Human development destroys an area of forest equal in size to 550,000 football fields.

A monarch butterfly on its annual migration flies 700 miles (1,127 kilometers).

There are as many as 8,000 earthquakes strong enough to be felt. Fewer than three, on average, are powerful enough to do serious damage.

Two mice, a male and a female, meet and mate. We'll check in with them again soon ...

A giant pumpkin can gain 150 pounds (68 kilograms).

Moose antlers, the fastest-growing tissue of any mammal, can add 6 inches (15 centimeters) to their length.

In One Month . . .

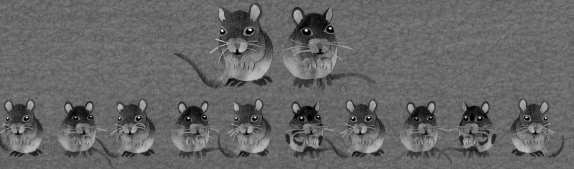

84,000 new books are published.

Our two mice had an average litter —10 babies. There are now 12 mice . . .

4,400,000 new cars leave the factory.

After the day, the month may be the oldest human unit of timekeeping. A month on our calendar is roughly based on the time it takes the moon to go through a full cycle of its phases, about 29½ days.

More than 700 new species of insects will be named.

The hair on a human head grows a half inch (1¼ centimeters).

People around the world produce enough trash to fill a square pit more than one mile (1,609 meters) on a side and 1,200 feet (366 meters) deep.

Human fingernails grow ⅛ of an inch (3 millimeters).

A eucalyptus tree can grow 30 inches (76 centimeters).

A migrating gray whale can cover 2,500 miles (4,023 kilometers) of open ocean.

The world's human population increases by about 6,556,000 people (11,616,000 are born and 5,060,000 die).

In One Year . . .

An estimated 50 people are killed by sharks.

More than 2,000,000 people are killed by mosquito-borne disease.

The moon moves one and a half inches (4 centimeters) farther away from Earth.

The year is based on the time it takes for Earth to make one full circuit of the sun. Along with the day and the month, the year is one of the three basic units of time shared by people throughout history.

An arctic tern flies 40,000 miles (64,000 kilometers) — the longest migration in the animal world.

Mount Everest rises half an inch (1¼ centimeters).

If all of the offspring of our original pair of mice survived and mated, the two rodents would now have more than 1,000,000 living descendants.

Humans cut down 4,000,000,000 trees.

A termite queen will lay almost 3,000,000 eggs.

There are 78,670,000 more people on earth (139,400,000 are born and 60,730,000 die).

Light travels 6,000,000,000,000 — six trillion — miles. This is one light-year.

Global warming causes a sea level rise of about ⅛ of an inch (3 millimeters).

Sea floor spreading moves the United States one inch (2½ centimeters) away from Europe.

Very Quick . . .

A housefly can spot danger and take off in $\frac{1}{10}$ of a second.

Light travels a distance equal to the length of Earth's equator in $\frac{1}{7}$ of a second.

A puff adder can strike and return to a coiled position in less than $\frac{1}{2}$ of a second.

In our universe some things — such as light traveling across a room — happen much too quickly for us to notice. Science has given us the ability to measure many of these very fast events, even if we can't experience them directly.

Dolphins can "see" using sound by making a series of clicks — each one as short as $\frac{1}{600}$ of a second — and listening to the echoes.

A fastball makes the trip from a major-league baseball pitcher's hand to home plate in less than $\frac{4}{10}$ of a second.

The human brain can register a finger touching something in $\frac{1}{100}$ of a second.

The trap-jaw ant snaps its jaws shut in $\frac{1}{800}$ of a second — the fastest movement in the animal world.

The Shasta salamander — an amphibian with the world's fastest tongue — can snap up an insect in $\frac{1}{100}$ of a second.

Very Long . . .

Observing the most distant galaxies is like peering into the distant past — we are seeing them as they were more than 13,000,000,000 years ago.

An object the size of the asteroid that may have killed off the dinosaurs collides with our planet about once every 100,000,000 years.

It would take 80,000 years for a spacecraft to reach the nearest star outside our solar system. A voyage across our galaxy would last almost 2,000,000,000 years.

On a human time scale, some events occur very rarely. Others seem to take place at an impossibly slow pace . . .

Counting one number every second, it would take more than 31,000 years to count to one trillion.

A French woman lived to be 122 years old. She holds the record for a human life span.

The sun will get larger and hotter. In 1,000,000,000 years, Earth will be too hot to support life as we know it. 2,000,000,000 years from now, Earth's oceans will have boiled away.

A koi — a kind of goldfish — lived to 226 years of age.

An ocean quahog, a clam, lived to be 405 years old — an animal world record.

The oldest living single organism we know of, a bristlecone pine in California, is more than 4,862 years old.

By the year 2100, it is predicted that sea levels worldwide will have risen about 19 inches (48 centimeters).

A History of the Universe

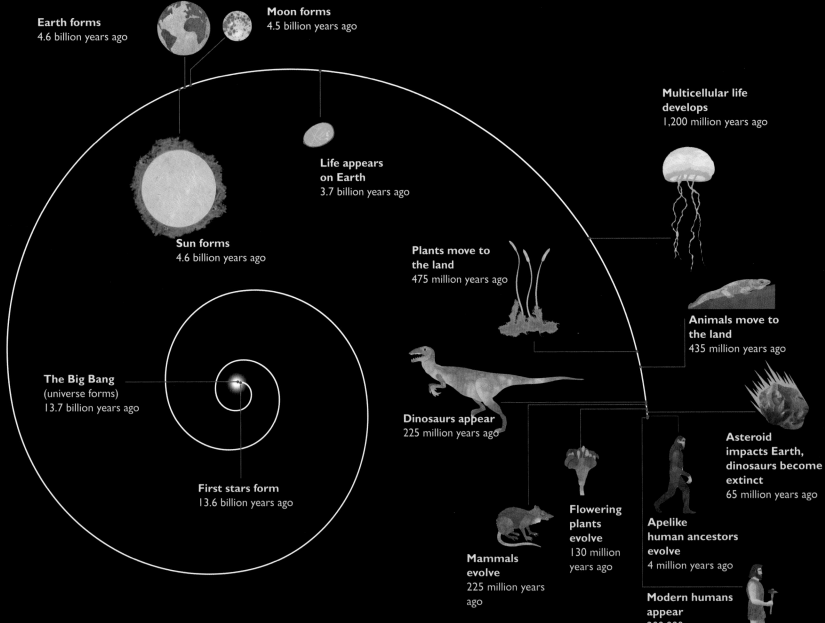

Earth forms
4.6 billion years ago

Moon forms
4.5 billion years ago

Multicellular life develops
1,200 million years ago

Life appears on Earth
3.7 billion years ago

Sun forms
4.6 billion years ago

Plants move to the land
475 million years ago

Animals move to the land
435 million years ago

The Big Bang
(universe forms)
13.7 billion years ago

Dinosaurs appear
225 million years ago

Asteroid impacts Earth, dinosaurs become extinct
65 million years ago

First stars form
13.6 billion years ago

Flowering plants evolve
130 million years ago

Apelike human ancestors evolve
4 million years ago

Mammals evolve
225 million years ago

Modern humans appear
200,000 years ago

Earth's Human Population: 1750 to 2050

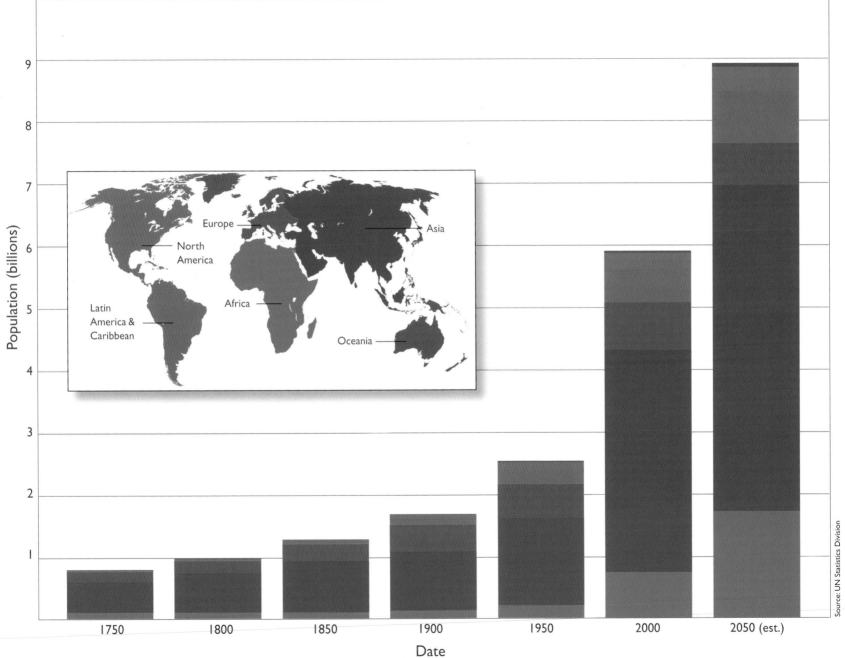

Population (billions)

Date

1750 1800 1850 1900 1950 2000 2050 (est.)

Europe
North America
Asia
Africa
Latin America & Caribbean
Oceania

Source: UN Statistics Division

Life Spans: How Long Do Plants and Animals Live?

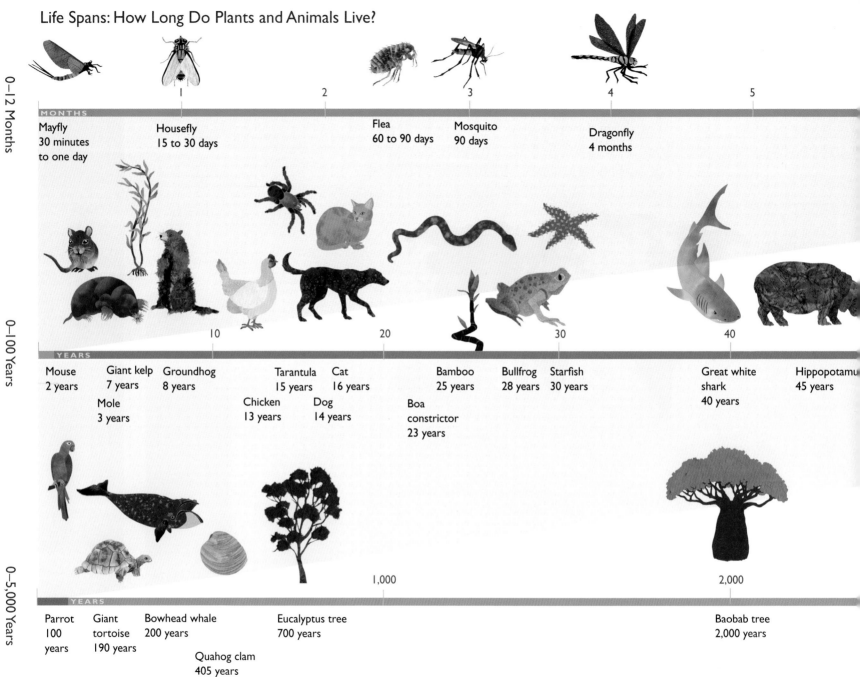

0–12 Months

MONTHS

1   2   3   4   5

Mayfly
30 minutes
to one day

Housefly
15 to 30 days

Flea
60 to 90 days

Mosquito
90 days

Dragonfly
4 months

0–100 Years

YEARS

10   20   30   40

Mouse
2 years

Giant kelp
7 years

Groundhog
8 years

Mole
3 years

Tarantula
15 years

Chicken
13 years

Cat
16 years

Dog
14 years

Bamboo
25 years

Boa
constrictor
23 years

Bullfrog
28 years

Starfish
30 years

Great white
shark
40 years

Hippopotamu
45 years

0–5,000 Years

YEARS

1,000   2,000

Parrot
100
years

Giant
tortoise
190 years

Bowhead whale
200 years

Quahog clam
405 years

Eucalyptus tree
700 years

Baobab tree
2,000 years

7   8   9   10   11   12

Worker ant
months

Monarch butterfly
4 weeks to 8 months

Bumblebee
12 months

60   70   80   90   100

Crocodile
55 years

Elephant
65 years

Human
(world average)
69 years

Blue whale
90 years

Lobster
100 years

3,000   4,000   5,000

Giant redwood
2,700 years

Bald cypress
3,500 years

Bristlecone pine
4,800 years

The History of Time and Timekeeping: Some Important Dates

30,000 B.C. to 10,000 B.C.	People make marks on pieces of wood to keep track of the moon's cycles. These are the first known calendars.
2500 B.C.	The Egyptians build tall, four-sided towers called obelisks. They use the shadow cast by these towers to keep track of time during the day.
2000 B.C.	The Babylonians introduce the idea of the second.
2000 B.C.	The Egyptians begin to divide the daytime and nighttime into twelve equal periods each. These periods are the ancestors of our hour, though their length changes as days grow longer or shorter with the seasons.
1500 B.C.	The sundial is developed in Egypt. Around the same time, the Egyptians also invent the water clock, which can keep track of time at night. Water dripping at a regular rate from one container to another indicates how much time had passed.
334 B.C.	Minutes and seconds are introduced to the Western world with the conquest of Babylon — what is now Iraq — by the Greek king Alexander the Great.
500	The Chinese are using candle clocks — marked candles that burn at a regular, known rate.
1000	The Chinese build three-story-tall, elaborate mechanical clocks that keep track of and predict astronomical events.
1475	The first clock with a minute hand is mentioned in a European manuscript.
1560	The first clock with a second hand is built in Germany. It is not very accurate.
1582	The Gregorian calendar — our modern calendar — is introduced in Europe.
1600s	Astronomers define the second as 1/86,400 of a day. But the speed of the earth's rotation, and thus the length of a day, varies, so not all seconds are the same length.
1721	The English clock maker George Graham makes a pendulum clock that gains or loses only one second each day.
1895	Daylight Savings Time is introduced in the United States, originally to save lighting costs. Daylight Savings Time shifts the clock so that it gets dark an hour later in the summer.
1905	Albert Einstein's Special Theory of Relativity shows that time is relative — it can move at different rates in different locations or when two observers are traveling at different speeds.
1945	The time unit *shake* is introduced. A unit of time used in computing and nuclear physics, it is 10 nanoseconds, or 10 billionths of a second.
1956	Astronomers decide to define the second as a fraction (1/31,556,926) of a year. The length of a year also varies slightly, so they use the year 1900 to make everyone's second the same length.
1967	Scientists agree to define a second as the time it takes for a cesium atom's electrons to go through exactly 9,192,631,770 cycles.
2010	A new atomic clock — the most accurate ever built — will gain or lose less than one second in three billion (3,000,000,000) years.

Additional Reading

The Book of Comparisons by The Diagram Group.
    London: Sidgwick & Jackson, 1980.

Eyewitness: Time & Space by John Gribbin.
    London: Dorling Kindersley, 2000.

In Search of Time: The Science of a Curious Dimension by Dan Falk.
    New York: Thomas Dunne Books, 2008.

The Story of Time by Kristen Lippincott.
    London: Merrell Holberton, 1999.

Time's Pendulum: From Sundials to Atomic Clocks, the Fascinating History of Timekeeping and How Our Discoveries Changed the World by Jo Ellen Barnett. New York: Harcourt Brace/Harvest Book, 1999.

A note about the facts and figures in this book . . .

The information in this book comes from a variety of printed and Internet sources. Some facts are well established — we know, for example, precisely how fast light travels. Others are estimates — there is no way to know exactly how many babies are born each day or how many trees are cut down in a year. In these cases, I've used multiple credible sources. When different figures are given for the same phenomena, I've generally used values in the middle of a range.